3-D DOT-TO-DOT
DINOSAURS

ARCTURUS

King of the Dinosaurs

Tyrannosaurus rex, or T. rex, lived 70 million years ago and was one of the largest meat-eating dinosaurs. It had a huge head, 50 razor-sharp teeth and a long, heavy tail.

Mighty Meat-eater

Giganotosaurus was a mighty hunter that lived 90 million years ago. It was even bigger than T. rex but its brain was much smaller. Some of its teeth were as long as bananas!

Spiny Predator

Spinosaurus was possibly the largest of the meat-eating dinosaurs. It had a huge sail on its back. This was made of spines covered in skin, which may have helped to attract mates or frighten predators.

Duck-billed Giant

Parasaurolophus could walk on two or four legs. It was a herbivore, so it only ate plants. It had a long, curved tube on its skull that scientists think it used to make noises.

Fearsome Flyers...

The pterosaurs were flying reptiles. Tapejera was a fish-eating pterosaur with an enormous head and a spectacular crest. Pterosaurs could be as tiny as blackbirds or as big as small planes!

...the Pterosaurs

This amazing pterosaur, Quetzalcoatlus, was probably the biggest creature that has ever flown. Its wingspan was huge and it could glide without flapping its wings. It was a flying monster!

Monster of the Deep

Pliosaurs were swimming reptiles. One of these, Liopleurodon, was very long and built for speed. It was twice the length of a killer whale today. This fierce predator had lots of needle-sharp teeth.

Underwater Terror

Ophthalmosaurus was an ichthyosaur, another type of underwater reptile. It spent its life in water, had large eyes and a long jaw. Scientists think that it could hold its breath for 20 minutes!

Gentle Giants...

Brachiosaurus was very long and used its neck to reach leaves in the treetops. It had a small head and a tiny brain. It spent most of its time looking for food and its teeth were shaped like spoons.

...the Plant-eaters

Supersaurus was another enormous plant-eating dinosaur. Like other big plant-eaters, it swallowed its food whole in order to eat more quickly. These huge dinosaurs would eat all day long!

Early Bird

Archaeopteryx is thought to have been the first bird. Scientists have found that it had feathers like a bird but a long, bony tail like a reptile. It lived around 150 million years ago and was the size of a chicken.

Mini Monster

Saltopus was one of the first dinosaurs on Earth and one of the smallest meat-eaters. It was only just bigger than a cat, but could run fast to catch its prey or to escape larger predators!

Tough Customer

Triceratops looked very threatening with its big body, thick legs and three sharp horns. In fact, it only ate plants and T. rex would have been one of its most dangerous predators.

Well Protected

Stegosaurus had many bony plates on its back. They may have been used to keep it warm, or cool it down. There were other well protected dinosaurs, too. They had hard plates, spikes, small horns and tail clubs.

Awesome Hunter

Albertosaurus was the top predator of its time.
It was much smaller than its relative T. rex, which lived
millions of years later. It could run very fast on
two back legs and had a huge head.

This edition published in 2013 by Arcturus Publishing Limited
26/27 Bickels Yard, 151–153 Bermondsey Street,
London SE1 3HA

Copyright © 2013 Arcturus Publishing Limited

ISBN: 978-1-78212-208-1
CH002730EN
Supplier 01, Date 0313, Print Run 2480
Printed in Malaysia